AUTHOR'S INTRODUCTION

When I started work on this book in mid-1988, I hoped
to have it finished and published in time for the
anniversary of the outbreak of World War Two.
What I did not know then was that fate had other plans
and would hold things up until the right publisher came
along.
That happened when I was given a copy of Peter
Warnett's delightful book, 'Three Mile Man', and I
realised from looking at the little map inside that while
Peter was away at the war, I had been an evacuee
living on, roaming around, and eventually working on his
precise patch.
I knew then that a benign fate had pushed me gently
towards his publishers near Uckfield, Sweethaws Press.
No doubt, the village of Rotherfield will have recognised
itself by now, and when it goes through my book, I hope
it will show some forbearance over any liberties I may
have taken with its faces, places, architecture and
landscapes, and accept my excuse that it was drawn
from memory and out of love for the place, and without
any reference other than some old photographs given to
me by Duncan Goulding, the son of my first 'billet'
people.
I make no apologies whatsover for sneaking a look in
the archives to draw some Battle of Britain aeroplanes.

Chic Jacob

A
Boy's Own
War

Written and Illustrated by
Chic Jacob

Foreword by Derek Jameson

ACKNOWLEDGEMENTS

I would like to thank not a few of my youngish friends at the
Observer, and Sheena Boyd, one-time art Editor of *Punch,* for
prodding me into getting on with this book.
I'd particular like to thank Barbara Willard for straightening
out a word or two, Edie Reilly for processing them all, and
my dear friend, Jane Bown, for taking a spiffing photograph.
A nod, too, in the direction of those old evacuee chums I met
recently, who corroborated stories and jostled a memory or
two.
But most of all I would like to thank Frank Burkhill, our old
music and French master, for giving me the only drawing
lesson I ever had in my life, and for teaching all of us to sing
so many lovely songs in so many different languages, and for
being the sort of teacher that every school in the land should
have.

Published in 1990 by
Sweethaws Press
Owl House
Poundgate
Near Uckfield
Sussex TN22 4DE
Telephone. Crowborough (0892) 653722

A CIP catalogue record for this book is available
from the British Library.

ISBN 0 9511795 3 5

Printed in Great Britain by BPCC Wheatons Ltd.
Hennock Road, Marsh Barton, Exeter EX2 8RP

Foreword

September 1, 1939 — at the time the most exciting day of our lives for us Cockney kids. War was imminent and the first priority was to get the children out of London and other big cities to the safety of the countryside.

A wise move. The Nazi blitz on Guernica in the Spanish Civil War had given the world a chilling preview of the aerial bombardment to come. In the event, more civilians were to die from Hitler's bombs than on the battlefield.

My friend Chic Jacob has captured the spirit of those times brilliantly in this delightful book recalling his own wartime experiences.

It is all here, just as the three million of us evacuated that hot September remember with such mixed emotions — affection for the kindly country folk who took us in, sadness to have been uprooted from our families.

We were in the thick of it all — a bunch of kids from Detmold Road Elementary School, clutching our gas masks in their square cardboard boxes. Too young to fight, old enough to know what was going on.

Chic's drawings tell the story. Boy's Own War it certainly was. Halcyon times, despite the horrors around us. Five-barred gates, fields of corn, real rabbits and cows, market days and church halls, GIs sounding like Hollywood films, dogfights in the sky.

Thanks, Chic, for bringing it back to life with such warmth and wit. Those who were there will never forget it. As for the rest, sit back and enjoy a wonderful glimpse of life in what they called Britain's Finest Hour.

Derek Jameson

A Boy's Own War

For my grandchildren
Claire, Emily, Louise and Gemma
who live in a different world.

They took us from London to a place of safety some 20 miles south of Biggin Hill.

I got a ringside seat for the Battle of Britain and a love for the countryside.

The end of scout camp until another summer, so goodbye to Devon and the sea and sands of that southern coast.

The *8th Forest Hill Scout Troop* was on its way home to London, helped by huge doorstep jam sandwiches, bottles of Tizer, bursts of campfire song . . . Did any of us think about the date? Why should we. In fact it was the end of August 1939.

Mum met the tired lot of us when we reached home. There were piles of sandbags about. There was going to be a war, Mum said. It sounded exciting. But there was something more. With my two younger brothers I was to be sent away — 'To a place of safety,' she explained. 'The country. You'll like the country, won't you?'

Better than going back to school, thought I!

It was a bit like setting off on holiday. Lots of our schoolmates clambered on to the train with us. It was a proper train, a steam train, none of your London Underground or District Line. The only thing that seemed a bit funny, somehow, was that we all wore labels with our names and destination clearly marked — and we carried a square cardboard box on a string. Inside was our very own gas mask . . .

We piled aboard. The Guard was looking at his watch. Parents and friends stood back as doors slammed and the engine huffed. The whistle blew, the wheels turned. We were off. We waved, cheered, shouted GOODBYE! What a lark! Only a few small kids cried.

Mum had said to thank the engine driver for a safe journey. We let our baby brother do that . . .

Now we were in the country, in Sussex. 'Sussex, Sussex by the Sea' was a song we'd heard — but there wasn't a sniff of salt or a sign of a wave. The bus carried us up a hill, round a corner, by a sweetshop, on till we came to the cosy little red-brick village school. They were waiting for us — ladies in green uniforms, hats, twin-sets, brogues; and others wearing floral pinnies and rosy cheeks to match. There was a new sound as Sussex voices mixed with our shrill cockney and the posh accents of the ladies in green.

At last billets had been found for everybody — except one boy waiting for 'a gentleman to take him to The Hall' — and we three brothers. When the gentleman arrived, the Chief Billeting Lady spoke to him urgently. She waved her hand in our direction. 'They are inseparable,' she said.

The gentleman may have hesitated a bit but he soon made up his mind. We clambered into his car and were whizzed off to his house. This was the countryside all right. Leafy lanes, beechwoods, pongy farms . . . The gentleman, we learned, was American, his wife who came out to meet us was Australian. There was a maid in cap and apron and the son of the house stood in the doorway and looked us over. He was a university student. Clever. We soon learned that he had built himself his own enormous telescope. It was the size of a huge drainpipe and stood not a stone's throw from the house.

The first days were like a dream holiday. We learned about poaching, sailed home-made boats on the pond, gazed at the stars through the telescope, gorged on great juicy blackberries, ours for the picking. Nobody could possibly want to go back to London.

Now the shock . . . Mr Chamberlain spoke on the wireless and said we were at war with Germany.

That evening the American gentleman gave us our first wartime duty. We were sent to sit with a terrified young Mum who had just arrived from London. She was alone with her two small children in a spooky old house that lay at the end of a dark and creepy lane. The owls hooted and the trees groaned as we made our torchlit way to the front-door . . . Boy! Was she glad to see us.

Even more evacuees arrived.

The village absorbed our big boys' school, a junior mixed school, several young ladies from a secretarial college, eight Polish girl refugees and one very large Austrian youth with the name of Baron Alexander Von der Osten-Sacken. He'd been beaten silly by the Nazis. We called him Sacha.

We were here to stay for what was called 'the duration'. We got a very superior house near the Rectory to use as a school. It had acres of gardens, huge stables, a glass conservatory and a balcony on the upstairs landing. Not a bit like our old, huge County Council School back in London.

The first job for the senior prefects was to dig slit trenches for use as air raid shelters.

They dug them in the school's sunken garden — and it was bloomin' hard going through solid Sussex sandstone.

School dinners were cooked by the ladies of the Women's Institute and served in the corrugated iron British Legion hut. We looked forward to the days when Mrs Boniface was in charge. She served up huge lumps of chewy chocolate pudding in steaming hot runny custard.

Brand new subject on the school curriculum — ballroom dancing. A co-educational activity with the Polish girls. Our music master got it going with the help of a local couple who'd won prizes for their terpsichorean skills. We danced to Joe Loss and Stephane Grappelli records played on the school's wind-up gramophone.

The music master made full use of that gramophone to fill our heads with Rachmaninov, Chopin, Beethoven and Debussy.

I could whistle most of Rachmaninov's 2nd Piano Concerto in C Minor, long before Noel Coward got hold of it for 'Brief Encounter'.

Our Australian lady discovered we could draw and she put my brother and me to work doing Christmas cards — at tuppence a time. We had a derelict junk-room as a studio. I did the line work — Indian ink on vellum, and my brother filled in the colours from his Woolworth's paint box.

We made enough tuppences to go into Tunbridge Wells and buy our Mum a super vase for Christmas.

Just after Christmas we changed billets. Our baby brother had gone back to London, like many of the smaller kids at that time.

My other brother and I left our American gentleman and his wife and we trudged through snow and slush to a gardener's lodge on the other side of the village. A little old man wearing a sack as an apron and sporting a fine waxed moustache and a little dewdrop on the end of his nose was sweeping a pathway to his big green gates. He nodded us round to the back door.

We took off our gumboots and put on our slippers, as we were told, then followed our new lady into the cosy warmth of her kitchen. We sat in large wooden chairs and drank hot, thick, milkless cocoa beside a glowing range into which she popped our soggy woollen gloves and balaclava helmets to dry.

We were in bed by eight o'clock; cocooned in goose feathers and warming our feet on hot house bricks wrapped in flannel that had come straight out of the kitchen oven. Mine fell out in the middle of the night, only just missing the chamber pot.

We got used to the sound of housebricks hitting wooden floors in the stillness of the blackout — and we made sure, in future, that our pot was always pushed well under the bed.

There was no bathroom at the Lodge. But on Friday nights my brother and I would put on our best clothes and go across the road to the Big House where 'The Colonel' lived in isolated splendour. He'd only a few domestic servants and a handful of gardeners to attend his needs. We'd follow The Colonel's butler up the stairs and down a long corridor to take a bath in the servants' quarters.

We had many a bath at The Colonel's house and spent many a day roaming his estates, but in all the time we were there, we never saw The Colonel once — and I'm sure he never saw us.

That first winter of the war in Sussex was pure joy. We had days off from school because it was too cold for lessons. A good supply of timber found in outbuildings and stables made us some pretty fair toboggans which we raced all day on the downhill slopes around the village. My hands got so wet and cold they tingled with a prickly glow.

A pond in the village froze over.

The owners of the pond opened their large five-barred gate and everyone poured in to have fun on the rock-solid ice. It was our first taste of 'wartime spirit'.

The winter was over and the war still seemed a million miles away. It was safe enough to bike to London and visit our parents.

Three hours to do the thirty miles up on a Saturday morning and two and three quarters to get back on Sunday night. We clipped fifteen minutes off the return journey by freewheeling down Poll Hill, heads down over the handlebars. We'd have been faster but my brother only had a small 20 inch wheel bike.

Our big brother was home on leave from the Fleet Air Arm. We went with him to see Auntie Maud in Dulwich. Auntie Maud was a court dressmaker and was altering our brother's Navy issue uniform for him.

She'd made it skin tight, which was just the way he wanted it. It was called making it 'tiddly'. All smart sailors had a 'tiddly' suit.

The boy scouts in the school got together and formed a troop. A real ragbag of an outfit with hardly any two uniforms the same.

We had some difficulty getting a scoutmaster though. They came in succession from nearby villages. None lasted for long, so we ran the show ourselves — Senior scout in charge.

The District Commissioner thought we couldn't — in fact he told us we shouldn't — but we did. He changed his mind later on and gave us his blessing when he saw we were doing it right — and having fun. I was third in line to run the troop after the two most senior scouts went home. I didn't have long to wait.

Best of all was camping on the scout reservation at Broadstone Warren. We'd cross Ashdown Forest loaded with tents, sleeping bags, billy cans and rations. We had our independence, and it gave our billet ladies a bit of a breather at weekends.

Our next door neighbours lived two hundred yards up the lane; two girls, the same age as my brother and me, their Mum and a small ginger haired evacuee from the junior school.

We were a gang. The girls taught us how to milk cows and round up cattle. The first cow I ever milked was a poor clapped-out old thing who needed her udder relieving before being sent off to market.

The girls' garden was stuffed full with rabbits, goats, chickens, cats and dogs, and vegetables growing in neat rows. Occasionally there'd be a pony or two for us to ride.

We were shown the George Cross their Dad had been awarded for pulling British airmen from a blazing plane that had crashed on the South Downs. He had been ploughing at the time.

A rival gang in our lane had been shown the Victoria Cross their billet man won in the First World War. He kept it in a tin box hidden up the chimney.

We were rounding up cattle with the girls when it started.

We heard the persistent droning of aircraft. It went on for an unusually long time. We were used to hearing an odd Anson or Blenheim stooging around at a fairly low level. But this was different.

We tilted our heads right back, blinked against the strong sunlight and focussed on something pretty awesome. Formations of German bombers and their fighter escorts on their way up the road to devastate Biggin Hill.

We heard the girls' Mum calling. We ran to their house and got under the stairs.

The dog fights went on for days. Run-of-the-mill collectors' items for kids were cartridge clips, cartridge cases and bits of shrapnel that fell out of the skies. Real kudos, though, was to get a bit of fabric from a German bomber. You had to be quick on your bike for that.

One German bomber narrowly missed the roof of the Lodge. It scraped the top of our pine trees and crashed a mile away. Our billet lady had our bikes locked up in her corrugated iron shed before we could say 'It's a Dornier!'

We watched two 'Spits' doing a victory roll over their kill.
My mate Malcolm got on his bike and grabbed a bit of Spandau machine gun that day. We were green with envy.

German bombers weren't the only planes to come down around the village. One Hawker Hurricane made a forced landing in 'Ten-acre field' behind our school.

My mate Malcolm was first on the scene and got the pilot's autograph. He was French, said Malcolm, because he wrote 'Bonjour Toto' on his scrap of paper. But the little old lady who gave the pilot a cup of tea said he was Polish.

We arrived late, only in time to see the airman heave his parachute into the back of a black Wolseley police car, then clamber in waving a piece of his plane's propellor as a souvenir. I reckon he was Polish.

On the most ferocious day of the battle, three of us stood on the top of Castle Hill and hurled a hugely defiant 'Land of Hope and Glory' at the vapour-drenched sky.

Malcolm wasn't with us. He was busy being shot at by a low-flying Messerschmitt. He had to dive into a ditch.

We got fairly used to it all.

Suddenly the daytime rattle of dogfighting stopped, to be replaced by the undulating drone of bombers in the night.

Some would jettison their loads before reaching London and we'd have days off school to help local farmers fill in the craters left behind.

One old farmer told us how he blasted at a German night bomber with his shotgun.

'I let the bugger have both barrels,' he said. 'And I heard they shots rattle against the side!'

No biking up to London now that 'the Blitz' was on.

We got ourselves some work at the weekends hoeing on a farm. Tuppence an hour — bring your own lunch.

Old Granny Grinham taught us how to go about it.

When the night bombing started, more evacuees arrived in the village including our billet lady's daughter and her two small children. They came from the Medway, which was under heavy attack. The small front parlour at the Lodge became their bedroom.

We were all happy together. There was never any talk of moving my brother and me elsewhere.

To our billet lady we were now 'her boys'.

Not long afterwards my brother went away to a nautical training school and that eased the crowded Lodge somewhat. He'd always wanted to go into the Navy.

Mum and Dad brought him down to show him off in his new 'school' uniform.

We thought the war would be over long before we were old enough to get involved, but my young brother 'signed on' and they had him on Russian convoys at the age of sixteen. He did three runs to Murmansk before the war in Europe ended.

Meanwhile our baby brother had been re-evacuated to Cornwall when the bombing of London started. He was now living happily in Liskeard, with a railwayman and his wife.

They invited the whole of our family down for a week's holiday. We were spread out in bedrooms all along the railway company's terrace of houses. Each house had its own barrel of home-made scrumpy fermenting in the back yard.

We had to watch with envy as our smirking baby brother puffed his way past us on the footplate of the local train when he went on his weekly Saturday treat down to Looe.

I returned to find the village awash with Canadian soldiers.

They rode magnificent Harley Davidson motorbikes, wore mansized crash helmets and had leather jerkins with their names and regimental insignia painted on the backs. We liked them.

We never saw any Yanks in our part of Sussex. The Canadians were our Yanks.

My one great dream was to get myself a pair of Canadian dispatch-riders' boots.

As an adjunct to the Home Guard we formed a unit of the Army Cadet Force. We wore the cap badge of the Sussex Regiment and were a mixture of local village lads and evacuees from London.

We marched up and down with wooden rifles and did our arms drill in the square. We played the Canadians at football and they taught us how to strip down Bren Guns.

The older boys were allowed to go on night manoeuvres with the Home Guard against the Canadians.

We carried messages from Home Guard Headquarters at the Kings Arms to the strategically placed defensive blockhouses around the village, and also to isolated units of old codgers nursing make-believe Molotov cocktails in sandbagged slit trenches.

Got my first drink in a pub with the Home Guard. Had to keep our heads down though, in case the local bobby 'P.C. Half-Hundred' was on the prowl.

Some young ladies got engaged to Canadians and lots of soldiers were invited in for tea by the villagers.

Two Canadians soldiers often came to the Lodge for tea. They were brothers. One day they brought their father along. He had joined the Canadian Army to be with them in England.

They called him 'Pop. We all called him 'Pop'.

Malcolm and I were sent down to Shornecliffe on the Kent coast to do a Physical Training Instructors course at an army barracks there. We had to have special passes to go on the bus through the military zone. It was August 1942.

Nearly all the other boys on the course were from Public Schools and couldn't play football for toffee.

That was their bad luck because all the Army Physical Training Instructors seemed to be professionals from well-known football teams.

Malcolm and I learned a lot from them.

There was a lot of air activity over the Straits of Dover (Hellfire Corner). We wondered why.

One night we lay in our beds listening to an almighty racket going on across the Channel.

Was it an air raid?

It seemed to go on too long for that.

I returned 'home' as proud as Punch, with my newly acquired Physical Training Instructor's insignia over my sergeant's stripes.

The Lodge was quiet and heavy with sadness. Both the Canadian brothers were dead — killed in action.

We'd been listening to the raid on Dieppe that night in the barracks on the Kent coast.

It was my first big shock of the war. Friends got killed.

Our school was shrinking in numbers. There were only two of us left in the sixth form. If I wanted to stay in the country I'd have to take my Oxford Schools Certificate. I didn't want to go home so I stayed and took the exam.

Most of our lessons were taken on elegant walks around the village lanes. We had masters queuing up to teach us things. We both passed. My sole classmate is now a Professor of Criminology at a leading university.

I lugged my bike and suitcase down to the station and went home by guard's van. My days as an evacuee were over.

Back home in London I got a job as a clerk at the GEC and hated it.

   The only pleasures I ever got were from watching 'our' girls playing netball in Lincoln's Inn Fields or listening to the Communist agitators on the corner calling for a second front.

   The Dame Myra Hess concerts at the National Gallery weren't bad either — if you could get in.

London was being buzz bombed now; but there was one audacious attack by yellow-nosed Messerschmitts.

They hedge-hopped their way up to South East London, machine-gunned my future wife in Peckham High Street, strafed our local barrage balloon and went on to bomb the local infants school — which must have looked like a factory to them. Our neighbour's little girl June had slipped out at playtime to buy her sweet ration. She didn't get killed that day.

I got browned off making out invoices at the GEC, so every Friday evening I'd get on my big brother's racing bike and go down to the farm for a couple of days real work . . .

On one of these weekend visits I made it known that I wouldn't half like a regular job with them.

We came to an agreement, the farmer and I. He would take me on as 'his pupil', which meant I'd get full board and lodging, precious little in the way of wages but I could stuff my head with as much agricultural knowledge as he could teach me.

We shook hands on it.

He said he'd soon have me knowing the difference between hay and a bull's foot.

First day they let me milk six cows before breakfast.

Whoopee!

I was taught to build haystacks and corn ricks, harness the horse, drive the cart, start the tractor, sit a binder, work the threshing machine and to use the tools of my trade proficiently — particularly pitchforks and hay knives.

We'd often go to local ploughing matches. Ploughmen would come from all over England with their great Shires and Percherons and Suffolk Punches. Usually the bow-legged men from Yorkshire walked off with the prizes.

They ate real ploughman's lunches — the end of a loaf, scrape of butter, wedge of cheese, raw onion and all washed down with cold tea swigged from a screwtop beer bottle.

We stopped work to watch formations of bombers flying overhead again, just as we'd done three years before in 1940.
This time they were going in the right direction — no need to run for shelter.
They were the big American Flying Fortresses we'd heard about, B17's on the first daylight mission to Germany.

I'd learnt enough as a farm pupil to get myself a job — with real wages.

I went to a 'posh' farm in Surrey owned by the man who was helping Lord Beaverbrook run the Ministry of Aircraft Production. I knew precious little about sheep, except that they were daft, but on the strength of this knowledge the farm bailiff made me his shepherd.

I had a real sheep dog and an old Romany caravan to sleep in during the lambing season, but the job didn't last long.

My eighteenth birthday was coming up. Time to go into the Armed Forces. I wanted to join my two brothers in the Royal Navy.

Some old toff interviewed me and let me know quite emphatically that it was up to him which branch of the Armed Services I would be sent into. He pooh-poohed my educational qualifications, sniffed when I told him I worked as a farm labourer and told me I was hardly suited to join the Navy's 'Y' scheme for the training of young officers as I'd suggested I might be.

He ticked me off for saying my brothers were serving on *HMS Victorious* and on *HMS Diadem* when surely I meant serving *in* those ships; but with a wan smile and an airy wave of his hand he put me down for the Navy.

Bully for him!

I was grateful though. He could have made me a Bevin Boy. Bevin Boys had to go to work down a coalmine.

One morning in May 1944 I boarded another train out of London, with a different set of lads. This time we were sent to the Butlins Holiday Camp at Skegness — at that time *HMS Royal Arthur*. We were kitted out and sent on to *HMS Glendower* at Pwllheli.

There we were taught the rudiments of seamanship, then shipped across to the Isle of Man for a course in radar, before going to St Mary's Gunnery School at Chatham to await our fate.

We were given embarkation leave. We were going abroad.

I went back to the village for a last look around with my billet-lady's grandchildren.

The *Reina del Pacifico,* a juddering old queen of a troopship, took us from Liverpool to Ceylon.

We went to a transit camp in the jungle just outside Colombo.

Lord Louis Mountbatten came and gave us a pep talk before we were dispersed around the fleet.

The war in Europe was ending. There was still the war with Japan to go.

But that's another story.

The *Reina del Pacifico,* a juddering old queen of a troopship, took us from Liverpool to Ceylon.

We went to a transit camp in the jungle just outside Colombo.

Lord Louis Mountbatten came and gave us a pep talk before we were dispersed around the fleet.

The war in Europe was ending. There was still the war with Japan to go.

But that's another story.